The Comprehensive Mediterranean Dishes Cookbook

Irresistible and On a Budget Recipes To Boost Your Brain

Alison Russell

to date, and reliable, complete information. No warranties of any kind are declared or implied. Readers acknowledge that the author is not engaging in the rendering of legal, financial, medical or professional advice. The content within this book has been derived from various sources. Please consult a licensed professional before attempting any techniques outlined in this book.

By reading this document, the reader agrees that under no circumstances is the author responsible for any losses, direct or indirect, which are incurred as a result of the use of information contained within this document, including, but not limited to, — errors, omissions, or inaccuracies.

Table of contents

Breakfast

Gingerbread Banana Bake with Quinoa

Preparation Time: 10 minutes

Cooking Time: 1 hour and 20 minutes

Servings: 2

Ingredients:

- Bananas, three cups, mashed
- Almonds, slivered, one-quarter cup
- Cinnamon, one tablespoon
- Milk, two and one-half cups
- Ginger, one teaspoon ginger
- Quinoa, one cup
- Salt, one-half teaspoon
- Allspice, one-half teaspoon, ground
- Cloves, one teaspoon, ground

Directions:

1. Heat the oven to 350.
2. Use oil spray on a nine by thirteen baking dish. Blend together the salt, vanilla, cloves, ginger, allspice, cinnamon, and bananas until smooth.
3. Stir in the milk and quinoa.
4. Pour this mixture into a baking dish and bake covered for one hour. After this, take it out of the oven and uncover.

5. Drizzle on sliced almonds and bake for another twenty minutes.

Nutrition:

Calories 213; 4 grams fat; 41 grams carbs; 18 grams sugar; 211 milligrams sodium; 4 grams fiber; 5 grams protein

Avocado and Feta Cheese Baked Eggs

Preparation Time: 25 minutes

Cooking Time: 15 minutes

Servings: 2

Ingredients:

- Salt and pepper, one-quarter of a teaspoon each
- Eggs, four
- Feta cheese, three tablespoons, crumbled finely
- Avocado, one large, cut into slices
- Olive oil, two tablespoons

Directions:

1. Heat the oven to 350. Lay the slices of avocado into two oven-safe personal-sized baking dishes.
2. Crack two of the eggs into each bowl easily, so you do not break the yoke.
3. Add the cheese crumbles and lightly sprinkle pepper and salt in each cup. Bake them for fifteen minutes.

Nutrition:

Calories 329

2.2 grams carbs

17 grams protein

Santa Fe Taco Salad

Preparation Time: 11 minutes

Cooking Time: 16 minutes

Servings: 2

Ingredients

Toppings:

- ½ pound 93 percent lean ground turkey (1 lean)
- 1/2 cup dried, rinsed, and drained black beans (1/2 healthy fat)
- Seasoned jalapeño chili pepper (1/4 green)
- Beefsteak tomatoes, chopped (1/2 healthy fat)
- 1 Clove of garlic, minced and peeled (1/8 condiment)
- 3 tablespoons of chopped scallions (1/2 green)
- 2 tablespoons of fresh cilantro chopped, plus garnish (1/2 green)
- Salt and ground black pepper, sweet paprika to taste 1 ¼ teaspoon (1/8 condiment)

For the Avocado Dip:

- ¼ cup, 2% Greek yogurt (1/2 healthy fat)
- ¼ cup of water (1/2 condiment)
- 1 medium avocado, peeled, pitted, chopped, and split (1/2 healthy fat)
- 1 ½ spoonful of fresh cilantro (1/4 green)
- ½ tablespoon cayenne pepper (1/8 condiment)

13

- Salt and black chili pepper, to taste (1/8 condiment)

For the Salad:

- 5 cups shredded iceberg lettuce cup shredded (1 green)
- 1 Mexican cheese mixed beefsteak tomato, chopped (1/2 healthy fat)
- Tablespoons of fresh coriander (1/2 green)
- 2 spoons smashed tortilla chips (1/2 healthy fat)

Directions:

1. Heat a broad skillet over medium-high heat, without sticking. Use a wooden spoon to split the meat into small pieces and add the ground turkey to the skillet. Cook, stirring constantly, for 4 to 5 minutes until the meat is no longer pink.

2. Incorporate beans, jalapeño, onions, garlic, scallions, salt, pepper, and paprika. Reduce heat to low, cover, and cook for 15 minutes. Remove the lid from the skillet and cook for about 5 minutes until the liquid decreases.

3. In the meantime, make the avocado dip: add yogurt, sugar, half the avocado, cilantro, cayenne, salt, and pepper into a blender. Up to a smooth process; reserve.

4. Divide the lettuce into 4 slabs. Top with the mixture of beef, cheese, onions, cilantro, and chopped

avocado left over. Add the avocado dip over the top and garnish the chips with crushed tortilla.

Nutrition:

491 calories

28g fat

11g protein

Mushroom and Spinach Omelet

Preparation Time: 3 minutes

Cooking Time: 15 minutes

Servings: 2

Ingredients:

- Olive oil, one tablespoon
- Green onion, one, diced finely
- Red onion, one-quarter of a cup, diced finely
- Egg, three
- Spinach, one and one-half fresh, chopped small
- Feta cheese, one-half of a cup, crumbled small
- Button mushrooms, five, sliced thinly

Directions:

1. Sauté the onions, mushrooms, and spinach for three minutes in the olive oil and then set them to the side.
2. Pour the well-beaten eggs into the skillet.
3. Let the eggs cook for three to four minutes until the edges begin to brown.
4. Sprinkle all of the other ingredients onto half of the omelet and then fold the other half over the ingredients.
5. Cook the omelet for one minute on each side.

Nutrition:

Calories 337; 25 grams fat; 911 milligrams sodium; 5.4 grams carbs; 1 gram fiber; 1.3 grams sugar; 22 grams protein

18

Fruit Bulgur

Preparation Time: 5 minutes

Cooking Time: 10 minutes

Servings: 2

Ingredients:

- 2 Cups Milk, 2%
- 1 ½ Cups Bulgur, Uncooked
- ½ Teaspoon Cinnamon
- 2 Cups Dark Sweet cherries, Frozen
- 8 Figs, Dried & Chopped
- ½ Cup Almonds, Chopped
- ¼ Cup Mint, Fresh & Chopped
- ½ Cup Almonds, Chopped
- Warm 2% Milk to Serve

Directions:

1. Get out a medium saucepan and combine your water, cinnamon, bulgur and milk together.

2. Stir it once and bring it just to a boil. Once it begins to boil then cover it, and then reduce your heat to medium-low. Allow it to simmer for ten minutes. The liquid should be absorbed.

3. Turn the heat off, but keep your pan on the stove. Stir in your frozen cherries. You don't need to thaw them, and then ad din your almonds and figs. Stir well before covering for a minute.

4. Stir your mint in, and then serve with warm milk drizzled over it.

Nutrition:

Calories: 301

Protein: 9 Grams

Fat: 6 Grams

Carbs: 57 Grams

Sodium: 40 mg

Mediterranean Toast

Preparation Time: 10 minutes

Cooking Time: 5 minutes

Servings: 2

Ingredients:

- 1 Slice Whole Wheat Bread
- 1 Tablespoon Roasted Red Pepper Hummus
- 3 Cherry Tomatoes, Sliced
- ¼ Avocado, Mashed
- 3 Greek Olives, Sliced
- 1 Hardboiled Egg, Sliced
- 1 ½ Teaspoons Crumbled Feta Cheese, Reduced Fat

Directions:

1. Start by topping your toast with ¼ avocado and then your hummus.
2. Add your remaining ingredients and season with salt and pepper before serving.

Nutrition:

Calories: 314

Protein: 4.2 Grams

Fat: 28.7 Grams

Carbs: 13.2 Grams

Sodium: 84 mg

Goat Cheese & Pepper Eggs

Preparation Time: 5 minutes

Cooking Time: 5 minutes

Servings: 2

Ingredients:

- 1 Cup Bell Pepper, Chopped
- 1 ½ Teaspoons Olive Oil
- 2 Cloves Garlic, Minced
- 6 Eggs, Large
- ¼ Teaspoon Sea Salt, Fine
- 2 Tablespoons Water
- ½ Cup Goat Cheese, Crumbled
- 2 Tablespoons Mint, fresh & chopped

Directions:

1. Start by getting a large skillet out and placing it over medium- high heat. Add in your oil. Once your oil begins to shimmer add in your peppers and allow them to cook for five minutes. Stir occasionally, and then add in your garlic and cook a minute more.

2. While your peppers cook whisk your slat, water and eggs together. Turn the heat to medium-low. Pour your egg mixture over the peppers, and then let them cook for about two minutes without stirring them. They should set on the bottom before you sprinkle your goat cheese over top.

3. Cook your eggs for another two minutes, and then serve with fresh mint.

Nutrition:

Calories: 201

Protein: 15 Grams

Fat: 15 Grams

Carbs: 5 Grams

Sodium: 166 mg

Mediterranean Egg Cups

Preparation Time: 15 minutes

Cooking Time: 25 minutes

Servings: 2

Ingredients:

- Bell pepper, one cup chopped finely
- Feta cheese, three tablespoons crumbled small
- Mushrooms, one cup chopped finely
- Eggs, ten
- Black pepper, one-quarter of a teaspoon
- Milk, two-thirds of a cup
- Salt, one-quarter of a teaspoon
- Garlic powder, one teaspoon
- Spray oil

Directions:

1. Heat the oven to 350. Spray oil in the twelve-muffin cup pan. Add the pepper, salt, garlic powder, and milk into the beaten egg until mixed well.
2. Add in the peppers and the mushrooms.
3. Fill the muffin pan cups with this mix. Bake for twenty-five minutes. Cool for five minutes then top with the cheese and serve.

Nutrition:

Calories 67

4.7 grams fat

Sodium 161.4 milligrams

1.2 grams carbs

.7 grams sugar

4.6 grams protein

Breakfast Egg on Avocado

Preparation Time: 10 minutes

Cooking Time: 15 minutes

Servings: 2

Ingredients:

- 1 tsp. garlic powder
- 1/2 tsp. sea salt
- 1/4 cup Parmesan cheese (grated or shredded)
- 1/4 tsp. black pepper
- 3 medium avocados (cut in half, pitted, skin on)
- 6 medium eggs

Directions:

1. Prepare muffin tins and preheat the oven to 350oF.
2. To ensure that the egg would fit inside the cavity of the avocado, lightly scrape off 1/3 of the meat.
3. Place avocado on muffin tin to ensure that it faces with the top up.
4. Evenly season each avocado with pepper, salt, and garlic powder.
5. Add one egg on each avocado cavity and garnish tops with cheese.
6. Pop in the oven and bake until the egg white is set, about 15 minutes.
7. Serve and enjoy.

Nutrition:

Calories per serving: 252

Protein: 14.0g

Carbs: 4.0g

Fat: 20.0g

Multigrain Blueberry Yogurt Pancakes

Preparation Time: 10 minutes

Cooking Time: 20 minutes

Servings: 2

Ingredients:

- Blueberries, one cup, fresh
- Eggs, two
- Salt, one-quarter teaspoon
- Plain Greek yogurt, one cup
- Baking powder, one teaspoon and one tablespoon
- Milk, four tablespoons
- Barley or rye flour, one-quarter of a cup
- All-purpose flour, one-half of a cup
- Butter, three tablespoons, melted
- Wheat flour, one-half of a cup
- Lemon zest, one teaspoon
- Vanilla, one teaspoon

Directions:

1. Blend together the milk, eggs, yogurt, and butter.
2. Mix the dry ingredients together in a separate bowl.
3. Spoon the wet ingredients gently into the dry ingredients and blend.

4. Pour the batter, one-quarter of a cup for each pancake, into the hot skillet that has been oiled with a light coating of olive oil.
5. Cook each pancake for three to four minutes on each side.

Nutrition:

Calories 98, 3.2 grams fat, 141 milligrams sodium, 15 grams carbs, 1.7 grams fiber, 1.7 grams sugar, 3.1 grams protein

Lunch

Spanish-Style Lamb Chops

Preparation Time: 10 minutes

Cooking Time: 8 hours

Servings: 2

Ingredients:

- 1 teaspoon extra-virgin olive oil
- ½ cup diced onion
- ½ cup diced roasted red pepper
- 2 tablespoons fresh parsley
- ½ cup red wine
- 1/8 Teaspoon sea salt
- Freshly ground black pepper
- 1 teaspoon minced garlic
- ½ teaspoon minced fresh rosemary
- 1 teaspoon smoked paprika
- 2 bone-in lamb shoulders, trimmed of fat
- 2 red potatoes, unpeeled, quartered

Directions:

1. Grease the inside of the slow cooker with the olive oil.
2. Put the onion, red pepper, parsley, and wine into the slow cooker.

3. In a small bowl, combine the salt, a few grinds of the black pepper, garlic, rosemary, and paprika. Rub this mixture over the lamb chops.

4. For even better flavor, do this one day ahead to allow all the flavors of the rub to permeate the meat.

5. Place the chops into the slow cooker on top of the onion and wine mixture.

6. The chops may need to slightly overlap one another to fit. Place the potatoes on top of the lamb. Cover and cook on low for 8 hours.

Nutrition:

Calories: 419; Saturated Fat: 4g; Trans Fat: 0g; Carbohydrates: 43g; Fiber: 6g; Sodium: 326mg; Protein: 27g

Chicken Pesto Polenta

Preparation Time: 15 minutes

Cooking Time: 6 hours & 45 minutes

Servings: 6

Ingredients:

- 4 boneless, skinless chicken breasts, bite-sized pieces
- 1 cup prepared pesto, divided
- 1 medium onion, peeled and finely diced
- 4 cloves garlic, minced
- 11/2 teaspoons dried Italian seasoning
- 1 (16-ounce) tube prepared polenta, cut into 1/2" slices
- 2 cups chopped fresh spinach
- 1 (141/2-ounce) can diced tomatoes
- 1 (8-ounce) bag shredded low-fat Italian cheese blend

Directions:

1. Mix the chicken pieces with pesto, onion, garlic, and Italian seasoning in a large bowl. Layer half of the chicken mixture, half the polenta, half the spinach, and half the tomatoes in a greased 4- to 5-quart slow cooker.
2. Continue to layer, ending with tomatoes. Cover and cook on low within 4–6 hours or on high for 2–3

hours. Top with cheese. Cover and continue to cook for 45 minutes to an hour until cheese has melted.

Nutrition:

Calories: 535

Fat: 16g

Protein: 32g

Sodium: 429mg

Fiber: 4g

Carbohydrates: 65g

Sugar: 4g

Cilantro Beef

Preparation Time: 10 minutes

Cooking Time: 4.5 hours

Servings: 4

Ingredients:

- 1-pound beef loin, roughly chopped
- ¼ cup apple cider vinegar
- 1 tablespoon dried cilantro
- ½ teaspoon dried basil
- 1 cup of water
- 1 teaspoon tomato paste

Directions:

1. Mix meat with tomato paste, dried cilantro, and basil.
2. Then transfer it in the slow cooker.
3. Add apple cider vinegar and water.
4. Cook the cilantro beef for 4.5 hours on High.

Nutrition:

211 calories,

30.4g protein,

0.4g carbohydrates,

9.5g fat,

0.1g fiber,

81mg cholesterol,

66mg sodium,

412mg potassium

Sweet and Tangy Duck

Preparation Time: 15 minutes

Cooking Time: 4 hours & 4 minutes

Servings: 6

Ingredients:

- 1 (3-pound) duckling, skin removed
- 1 tablespoon olive oil
- 1/2 teaspoon kosher salt
- 1/2 teaspoon freshly ground black pepper
- 1/2 teaspoon red pepper flakes
- 2 cloves garlic, minced
- 1 medium apple, cut into 1" pieces
- 1 medium pear, peeled, slice into 1" pieces
- 1 tablespoon lemon juice
- 1 large red onion, peeled and chopped
- 1 large carrot, peeled and chopped
- 1 stalk celery, chopped
- 1/2 cup dry red wine
- 1/4 cup honey
- 1/4 cup cider vinegar
- 1 cup Roasted Chicken Broth

Directions:

1. Remove any extraneous fat from the duck. Cut into serving-size portions. Warm-up the olive oil in a

large skillet or Dutch oven until hot but not smoking. Add the duck and season with salt, pepper, and red pepper flakes.

2. Cook for 3 minutes on one side. Add garlic to the pan, flip the duck, and cook for 1 minute. While the duck is browning, place apple and pear pieces in a bowl of cold water with lemon juice.

3. Put the onion, carrot, and celery in the bottom of a 4- to 5-quart slow cooker. Drain the apple and pear, and top vegetables with the duck and apple and pear mixture.

4. In a small bowl, whisk the wine, honey, vinegar, and broth. Pour over the duck. Cover and cook on high within 3–4 hours.

Nutrition:

Calories: 422; Fat: 12g; Protein: 46; Sodium: 516mg; Fiber: 2g; Carbohydrates: 26g; Sugar: 19g

Beef and Scallions Bowl

Preparation Time: 10 minutes

Cooking Time: 5 hours

Servings: 4

Ingredients:

- 1 teaspoon chili powder
- 2 oz. scallions, chopped
- 1-pound beef stew meat, cubed
- 1 cup corn kernels, frozen
- 1 cup of water
- 2 tablespoons tomato paste
- 1 teaspoon minced garlic

Directions:

1. Mix water with tomato paste and pour the liquid in the slow cooker.
2. Add chili powder, beef, corn kernels, and minced garlic.
3. Close the lid and cook the meal on high for 5 hours.
4. When the meal is cooked, transfer the mixture in the bowls and top with scallions.

Nutrition:

258 calories,

36.4g protein,

10.4g carbohydrates,

7.7g fat,

2g fiber,

101mg cholesterol,

99mg sodium,

697mg potassium

Adobo Steak Fajitas

Preparation Time: 10 minutes

Cooking Time: 6 – 8 hours

Servings: 2

Ingredients:

- 1 tablespoon freshly squeezed lime juice
- 1 tablespoon minced garlic
- 2 tablespoons minced chipotles in adobo
- 1 tablespoon extra-virgin olive oil
- 1/8 Teaspoon sea salt
- 12 ounces skirt steak, sliced thin
- 2 bell peppers, assorted colors, cored and cut into thin strips
- ½ onion, halved and cut into thin half circles
- 4 corn tortillas
- 1 small avocado, sliced, for garnish

Directions:

1. In a small bowl, whisk together the lime juice, garlic, chipotles, olive oil, and salt. Add the skirt steak to the bowl and toss to thoroughly coat the meat. You can allow this to marinate overnight in the refrigerator if you wish.
2. Put the steak, peppers, and onions into the slow cooker.

3. Cover and cook on low for 6 to 8 hours. The vegetables and meat will be very tender.

4. Serve in warmed corn tortillas garnished with the avocado slices.

Nutrition:

Calories: 791, Saturated Fat: 12g, Trans Fat: 0g, Carbohydrates: 46g, Fiber: 15g, Sodium: 501mg, Protein: 52g

Classic Chicken Parmesan

Preparation Time: 15 minutes

Cooking Time: 4 hours & 13 minutes

Servings: 4

Ingredients:

- 1 large egg
- 1/2 cup bread crumbs
- 1/2 teaspoon dried basil
- 1/2 teaspoon dried oregano
- 6 (4-ounce) boneless, skinless chicken breast halves
- 1 tablespoon olive oil
- 13/4 cups Tomato Sauce
- 1/2 cup shredded mozzarella cheese
- 2 tablespoons grated Parmesan cheese
- 1/4 cup chopped fresh parsley

Directions:

1. Mix the egg until foamy in a shallow dish. Mix the bread crumbs, basil, and oregano in another shallow dish. Soak the chicken in the egg, then into the bread crumb mixture to coat.

2. Warm-up olive oil in a large skillet until hot but not smoking. Put the chicken and brown within 3 minutes. Flip, and cook again within 3 minutes.

3. Put the chicken in a 4- to 5-quart slow cooker. Cover with tomato sauce. Cook on high for 3–4 hours. Sprinkle with cheeses, turn heat to low, and cook for 10 minutes. Remove from slow cooker and garnish with parsley.

Nutrition:

Calories: 278, Fat: 11g, Protein: 32g, Sodium: 732mg, Fiber: 1.5g, Carbohydrates: 11g, Sugar: 4g

Korean-Style Short Ribs & Carrots

Preparation Time: 10 minutes

Cooking Time: 8 hours

Servings: 2

Ingredients:

- 1 tablespoon low-sodium soy sauce
- 1 tablespoon fish sauce
- 1 tablespoon rice wine vinegar
- 1 teaspoon Sriracha
- 1 teaspoon toasted sesame oil
- 1 teaspoon minced garlic
- 1 teaspoon minced fresh ginger
- 8 ounces short ribs, trimmed of fat
- 4 carrots, cut into 2-inch pieces
- 2 cups low-sodium beef broth
- 1 scallion, white and green parts, sliced thin, for garnish

Directions:

1. In a small bowl, whisk together the soy sauce, fish sauce, vinegar, Sriracha, sesame oil, garlic, and ginger. Spread this mixture onto the short ribs to coat thoroughly. You can do this one day ahead if you wish and keep the short ribs in the refrigerator.

2. Put the carrots into the slow cooker and then set the short ribs on top. Pour in the beef broth.
3. Cover and cook on low for 8 hours. To serve, garnish the short ribs with the scallions.

Nutrition:

Calories: 532; Saturated Fat: 18g; Trans Fat: 0g; Carbohydrates: 15g; Fiber: 3g; Sodium: 1293mg; Protein: 18g

Rotisserie-Style Chicken

Preparation Time: 15 minutes

Cooking Time: 5 hours & 15 minutes

Servings: 6

Ingredients:

- 1 (4-pound) whole chicken
- 11/2 teaspoons kosher salt
- 2 teaspoons paprika
- 1/2 teaspoon onion powder
- 1/2 teaspoon dried thyme
- 1/2 teaspoon dried basil
- 1/2 teaspoon ground white pepper
- 1/2 teaspoon ground cayenne pepper
- 1/2 teaspoon ground black pepper
- 1/2 teaspoon garlic powder
- 2 tablespoons olive oil

Directions:

1. In a small bowl, mix salt, paprika, onion powder, thyme, basil, white pepper, cayenne pepper, black pepper, plus garlic powder. Massage with the spice mixture the entire chicken.
2. Place the spice-rubbed chicken in a greased 6-quart slow cooker. Drizzle olive oil evenly over the chicken. Cook on high for 3–31/2 hours or on low for 4–5 hours. Remove chicken carefully from the

slow cooker and place on a large plate or serving platter.

Nutrition:

Calories: 400

Fat: 14g

Protein: 64g

Sodium: 820mg

Fiber: 0.5g

Carbohydrates: 1g

Sugar: 0g

Beef with Greens

Preparation Time: 15 minutes

Cooking Time: 8 hours

Servings: 3

Ingredients:

- 1 cup fresh spinach, chopped
- 9 oz. beef stew meat, cubed
- 1 cup Swiss chard, c hopped
- 2 cups of water
- 1 teaspoon olive oil
- 1 teaspoon dried rosemary

Directions:

1. Heat olive oil in the skillet.
2. Add beef and roast it for 1 minute per side.
3. Then transfer the meat in the slow cooker.
4. Add Swiss chard, spinach, water, and rosemary.
5. Close the lid and cook the meal on Low for 8 hours.

Nutrition:

177 calories,

26.3g protein,

1.1g carbohydrates,

7g fat,

0.6g fiber,

76mg cholesterol,

95mg sodium,

449mg potassium

Rosemary Chicken with Potatoes

Preparation Time: 15 minutes

Cooking Time: 4 hours & 10 minutes

Servings: 6

Ingredients:

- 1 tablespoon olive oil
- 2 pounds boneless, skinless chicken thighs
- 1/2 teaspoon kosher salt
- 1/2 teaspoon freshly ground black pepper
- 6 small red potatoes, halved
- 1 leek (white and pale green parts only), sliced into 1" pieces
- 6 sprigs rosemary, divided
- 1 garlic clove, minced
- 1/2 cup Roasted Chicken Broth
- 1/4 cup capers

Directions:

1. Warm-up the olive oil in a large skillet over medium heat until hot but not smoking. Put the chicken and massage with salt and pepper. Cook within 5 minutes on one side and flip. Cook for an additional 5 minutes.

2. Place the potatoes and leek into a 4- to 5-quart slow cooker. Top with 5 sprigs of rosemary and garlic. Place chicken thighs on the rosemary. Pour broth

55

over chicken and potatoes. Cover and cook on high within 3–4 hours. Put capers before serving, and garnish with remaining rosemary.

Nutrition:

Calories: 336

Fat: 9g

Protein: 33g

Sodium: 595mg

Fiber: 3g

Carbohydrates: 30g

Sugar: 2g

Grilled Fish on Lemon s

Preparation Time: 10 minutes

Cooking Time: 10 hours

Servings: 4

Ingredients:

- 4 (4-ounce) fish fillets, such as tilapia, salmon, catfish, cod, or your favorite fish
- Nonstick cooking spray
- 3 to 4 medium lemons
- 1 tablespoon extra-virgin olive oil
- ¼ teaspoon freshly ground black pepper
- ¼ teaspoon kosher or sea salt

Directions:

1. Using paper towels, pat the fillets dry and let stand at room temperature for 10 minutes. Meanwhile, coat the cold cooking grate of the grill with nonstick cooking spray, and preheat the grill to 400°F, or medium-high heat. Or preheat a grill pan over medium-high heat on the stove top.

2. Cut one lemon in half and set half aside. Slice the remaining half of that lemon and the remaining lemons into ¼-inch-thick slices. (You should have about 12 to 16 lemon slices.) Into a small bowl, squeeze 1 tablespoon of juice out of the reserved lemon half.

3. Add the oil to the bowl with the lemon juice, and mix well. Brush both sides of the fish with the oil mixture, and sprinkle evenly with pepper and salt.

4. Carefully place the lemon slices on the grill (or the grill pan), arranging 3 to 4 slices together in the shape of a fish fillet, and repeat with the remaining slices. Place the fish fillets directly on top of the lemon slices, and grill with the lid closed. (If you're grilling on the stove top, cover with a large pot lid or aluminum foil.) Turn the fish halfway through the cooking time only if the fillets are more than half an inch thick. (See tip for cooking time.) The fish is done and ready to serve when it just begins to separate into flakes (chunks) when pressed gently with a fork.

5. Ingredient tip: We use the 10-minute-per-inch rule for grilling, baking, broiling, or panfrying any type of fish, since fish fillet sizes vary so much. Measure the thickest part of your fish fillets to determine the cooking time, and check the fish a minute or two before the suggested cooking time is up to prevent dried-out or overcooked fish. The fish is done when it just begins to separate into flakes (chunks) when pressed gently with a fork. The safe internal temperature for fish and seafood is 145°F.

Nutrition:

Calories: 147; Total Fat: 5g; Saturated Fat: 1g; Cholesterol: 55mg; Sodium: 158mg; Total Carbohydrates: 4g; Fiber: 1g; Protein: 22g

Creamy Sea Bass

Preparation Time: 15 minutes

Cooking Time: 2 hours

Servings: 4

Ingredients:

- 1-pound sea bass fillets, boneless
- 1 teaspoon garlic powder
- ½ teaspoon Italian seasoning
- ½ teaspoon salt
- ¼ cup heavy cream
- 1 tablespoon butter

Directions:

1. In the slow cooker, mix the sea bass with the other ingredients.
2. Close the slow cooker lid and cook for 2 hours on High.

Nutrition:

Calories 231,

Fat 14.9,

Carbs 7.4,

Protein 24.2

Tuscan Tuna and Zucchini Burgers

Preparation Time: 5 minutes

Cooking Time: 10 minutes

Servings: 4

Ingredients:

- 3 slices whole-wheat sandwich bread, toasted
- 2 (5-ounce) cans tuna in olive oil, drained
- 1 cup shredded zucchini (about ¾ small zucchini)
- 1 large egg, lightly beaten
- ¼ cup diced red bell pepper (about ¼ pepper)
- 1 tablespoon dried oregano
- 1 teaspoon lemon zest
- ¼ teaspoon freshly ground black pepper
- ¼ teaspoon kosher or sea salt
- 1 tablespoon extra-virgin olive oil
- Salad greens or 4 whole-wheat rolls, for serving (optional)

Directions:

1. Crumble the toast into bread crumbs using your fingers (or use a knife to cut into ¼-inch cubes) until you have 1 cup of loosely packed crumbs. Pour the crumbs into a large bowl. Add the tuna, zucchini, egg, bell pepper, oregano, lemon zest,

62

black pepper, and salt. Mix well with a fork. With your hands, form the mixture into four (½-cup-size) patties. Place on a plate, and press each patty flat to about ¾-inch thick.

2. In a large skillet over medium-high heat, heat the oil until it's very hot, about 2 minutes. Add the patties to the hot oil, then turn the heat down to medium. Cook the patties for 5 minutes, flip with a spatula, and cook for an additional 5 minutes. Enjoy as is or serve on salad greens or whole-wheat rolls.

3. Ingredient tip: Think of black pepper as a spice, not just a partner to salt. Black pepper can perk up a dish with a bit of heat, but without overwhelming other flavors. For the best flavor, buy whole peppercorns and grind them in a pepper mill or coffee grinder. Or buy the plastic mills that already contain whole peppercorns (in the spice aisle).

Nutrition:

Calories: 191; Total Fat: 10g; Saturated Fat: 2g; Cholesterol: 72mg; Sodium: 472mg; Total Carbohydrates: 11g; Fiber: 2g; Protein: 15g

Luncheon Party Meal

Preparation Time: 20 minutes

Cooking Time: 4½ hours

Servings: 4

Ingredients:

- 1 (14½-oz.) can diced tomatoes, drained
- 1 C. red sweet pepper, seeded and chopped
- 1 C. zucchini, sliced
- 2 garlic cloves, minced
- ½ C. dry white wine
- 8 oz. frozen medium shrimp, thawed
- 8 Klamath olives, pitted and chopped roughly
- ¼ C. fresh basil, chopped
- 1 tbsp. olive oil
- 1½ tsp. fresh rosemary, chopped
- Salt, to taste
- 2 oz. feta cheese, crumbled

Directions:

1. In a lightly greased slow cooker, place the tomatoes, sweet pepper, zucchini, garlic and wine and mix well.
2. Set the slow cooker on "Low" and cook, covered for about 4 hours.
3. Uncover the slow cooker and stir in the shrimp.

4. Set the slow cooker on "High" and cook, covered for about 30 minutes.
5. Uncover the slow cooker and stir in the remaining ingredients.
6. Serve hot with the topping of feta cheese.

Nutrition:

Calories per serving: 206; Carbohydrates: 10.8g; Protein: 16.7g; Fat: 8.9g; Sugar: 5.5g; Sodium: 423mg; Fiber: 2.5g

Dinner

Roasted Trout Stuffed with Veggies

Preparation Time: 10 minutes

Cooking Time: 25 minutes

Servings: 2

Ingredients:

- 2 (8-ounce) whole trout fillets
- 1 tablespoon extra-virgin olive oil
- ¼ teaspoon salt
- 1/8 teaspoon black pepper
- 1 small onion, thinly sliced
- ½ red bell pepper
- 1 poblano pepper
- 2 or 3 shiitake mushrooms, sliced
- 1 lemon, sliced

Directions:

1. Set oven to 425ºF (220ºC). Coat baking sheet with nonstick cooking spray.
2. Rub both trout fillets, inside and out, with the olive oil. Season with salt and pepper.
3. Mix together the onion, bell pepper, poblano pepper, and mushrooms in a large bowl. Stuff half

of this mix into the cavity of each fillet. Top the mixture with 2 or 3 lemon slices inside each fillet.

4. Place the fish on the prepared baking sheet side by side. Roast in the preheated oven for 25 minutes

5. Pullout from the oven and serve on a plate.

Nutrition:

Calories 453,

22g fat,

49g protein

Lemony Trout with Caramelized Shallots

Preparation Time: 10 minutes

Cooking Time: 20 minutes

Servings: 2

Ingredients:

- Shallots:
- 1 teaspoon almond butter
- 2 shallots, thinly sliced
- Dash salt
- Trout:
- 1 tablespoon almond butter
- 2 (4-ounce / 113-g) trout fillets
- 3 tablespoons capers
- ¼ cup freshly squeezed lemon juice
- ¼ teaspoon salt
- Dash freshly ground black pepper
- 1 lemon, thinly sliced

Directions:

For Shallots

1. Situate skillet over medium heat, cook the butter, shallots, and salt for 20 minutes, stirring every 5 minutes.

For Trout

1. Meanwhile, in another large skillet over medium heat, heat 1 teaspoon of almond butter.
2. Add the trout fillets and cook each side for 3 minutes, or until flaky. Transfer to a plate and set aside.
3. In the skillet used for the trout, stir in the capers, lemon juice, salt, and pepper, then bring to a simmer. Whisk in the remaining 1 tablespoon of almond butter. Spoon the sauce over the fish.
4. Garnish the fish with the lemon slices and caramelized shallots before serving.

Nutrition:

Calories 344, 18g fat, 21g protein

Easy Tomato Tuna Melts

Preparation Time: 5 minutes

Cooking Time: 4 minutes

Servings: 2

Ingredients:

- 1 (5-oz) can chunk light tuna packed in water
- 2 tablespoons plain Greek yogurt
- 2 tablespoons finely chopped celery
- 1 tablespoon finely chopped red onion
- 2 teaspoons freshly squeezed lemon juice
- 1 large tomato, cut into ¾-inch-thick rounds
- ½ cup shredded Cheddar cheese

Directions:

1. Preheat the broiler to High.
2. Stir together the tuna, yogurt, celery, red onion, lemon juice, and cayenne pepper in a medium bowl.
3. Place the tomato rounds on a baking sheet. Top each with some tuna salad and Cheddar cheese.
4. Broil for 3 to 4 minutes until the cheese is melted and bubbly. Cool for 5 minutes before serving.

Nutrition:

Calories 244, 10g fat, 30g protein

Mackerel and Green Bean Salad

Preparation Time: 10 minutes

Cooking Time: 10 minutes

Servings: 2

Ingredients:

- 2 cups green beans
- 1 tablespoon avocado oil
- 2 mackerel fillets
- 4 cups mixed salad greens
- 2 hard-boiled eggs, sliced
- 1 avocado, sliced
- 2 tablespoons lemon juice
- 2 tablespoons olive oil
- 1 teaspoon Dijon mustard
- Salt and black pepper, to taste

Directions:

1. Cook the green beans in pot of boiling water for about 3 minutes. Drain and set aside.
2. Melt the avocado oil in a pan over medium heat. Add the mackerel fillets and cook each side for 4 minutes.
3. Divide the greens between two salad bowls. Top with the mackerel, sliced egg, and avocado slices.

4. Scourge lemon juice, olive oil, mustard, salt, and pepper, and drizzle over the salad. Add the cooked green beans and toss to combine, then serve.

Nutrition:

Calories 737,

57g fat,

34g protein

Hazelnut Crusted Sea Bass

Preparation Time: 10 minutes

Cooking Time: 15 minutes

Servings: 2

Ingredients:

- 2 tablespoons almond butter
- 2 sea bass fillets
- 1/3 cup roasted hazelnuts
- A pinch of cayenne pepper

Directions:

1. Ready oven to 425ºF (220ºC). Line a baking dish with waxed paper.
2. Brush the almond butter over the fillets.
3. Pulse the hazelnuts and cayenne in a food processor. Coat the sea bass with the hazelnut mixture, then transfer to the baking dish.
4. Bake in the preheated oven for about 15 minutes. Cool for 5 minutes before serving.

Nutrition:

Calories 468,

31g fat,

40g protein

Butter Green Peas

Preparation Time: 10 Minutes

Cooking Time: 3 Hours

Servings: 4

Ingredients:

- 1 cup green peas
- 1 teaspoon minced garlic
- 1 tablespoon butter, softened
- ½ teaspoon cayenne pepper
- 1 tablespoon olive oil
- ¾ teaspoon salt
- 1 teaspoon paprika
- 1 teaspoon garam masala
- ½ cup chicken stock

Directions:

1. In the slow cooker, mix the peas with butter, garlic and the other ingredients,
2. Close the lid then cook it for 3 hours on High.

Nutrition:

Calories 121, Fat 6.5, Fiber 3, Carbs 3.4, Protein 0.6

Hot Paprika Green Beans Mix

Preparation Time: 10 minutes

Cooking Time: 1 hour

Servings: 4

Ingredients:

- 2 pounds shrimp, peeled and deveined
- ½ pound green beans, trimmed and halved
- 1 tablespoon avocado oil
- ½ cup low-sodium veggie stock
- 1 tablespoon tomato juice
- ½ cup red onion, chopped
- 1 teaspoon hot paprika
- 2 tablespoons cilantro, chopped

Directions:

1. In the slow cooker, combine the shrimp with the green beans, oil and the other ingredients, put the lid on and cook on High for 1 hour.
2. Divide into bowls and serve.

Nutrition:

Calories 301, Fat 4.4g, Cholesterol 478mg, Sodium 604mg, Carbohydrate 9.6g, Fiber 2.4g, Sugars 1.7g, Protein 53g, Potassium 546mg

Lemon Asparagus

Preparation Time: 8 Minutes

Cooking Time: 5 Hours

Servings: 2

Ingredients:

- 8 oz asparagus
- ½ cup butter
- Juice of 1 lemon
- Zest of 1 lemon, grated
- ½ teaspoon turmeric
- 1 teaspoon rosemary, dried

Directions:

1. In your slow cooker, mix the asparagus with butter, lemon juice and the other ingredients and close the lid.
2. Cook the vegetables on Low for 5 hours. Divide between plates and serve.

Nutrition:

Calories 139,

Fat 4.6.,

Fiber 2.5,

Carbs 3.3,

Protein 3.5

Lime Green Beans

Preparation Time: 10 Minutes

Cooking Time: 2 Hours and 30 Minutes

Servings: 5

Ingredients:

- 1-pound green beans, trimmed and halved
- 2 spring onions, chopped
- 2 tablespoons lime juice
- ½ teaspoon lime zest, grated
- 2 tablespoons olive oil
- ¼ teaspoon ground black pepper
- ¾ teaspoon salt
- ¾ cup of water

Directions:

1. In the slow cooker, mix the green beans with the spring onions and the other ingredients and close the lid.
2. Cook for 2.5 hours on High.

Nutrition:

Calories 67, Fat 5.6, Fiber 2, Carbs 4, Protein 2.1

Quinoa and Tomatillos Casserole

Preparation Time: 10 minutes

Cooking Time: 4 hours

Servings: 4

Ingredients:

- 1 cup low-fat Swiss cheese, shredded
- 12 ounces tomatillos, chopped
- 1 red bell pepper, chopped
- 1 pint cherry tomatoes, chopped
- ½ cup white onion, chopped
- 2 tablespoon oregano, chopped
- A pinch of black pepper
- 1 cup quinoa
- 1 tablespoon lime juice
- 2 pounds yellow summer squash, cubed
- Cooking spray

Directions:

1. In a bowl, mix the tomatoes with tomatillos, onion, lime juice and black pepper and toss.
2. Grease your slow cooker with the cooking spray and add quinoa.
3. Add half of the cheese and the squash and spread.
4. Add the rest of the cheese and the tomatillo mix, spread, cover and cook on Low for 4 hours.

5. Divide between plates, sprinkle oregano on top and serve.

Nutrition:

Calories 388, Fat 11.1g, Cholesterol 25mg, Sodium 203mg, Carbohydrate 50.1g, Fiber 10.1g, Sugars 8.3g, Protein 21.1g, Potassium 800mg

Roasted Shrimp-Gnocchi Bake

Preparation Time: 10 minutes

Cooking Time: 20 minutes

Servings: 4

Ingredients:

- 1 cup chopped fresh tomato (about 1 large tomato)
- 2 tablespoons extra-virgin olive oil
- 2 garlic cloves, minced (about 1 teaspoon)
- ½ teaspoon freshly ground black pepper
- ¼ teaspoon crushed red pepper
- 1 (12-ounce) jar roasted red peppers, drained and coarsely chopped
- 1-pound fresh raw shrimp (or frozen and thawed shrimp), shells and tails removed
- 1-pound frozen gnocchi (not thawed)
- ½ cup cubed feta cheese (about 2 ounces)
- 1/3 cup fresh torn basil leaves

Directions:

1. Preheat the oven to 425°F.
2. In a baking dish, mix the tomatoes, oil, garlic, black pepper, and crushed red pepper. Roast in the oven for 10 minutes.
3. Stir in the roasted peppers and shrimp. Roast for 10 more minutes, until the shrimp turn pink and white.

4. While the shrimp cooks, cook the gnocchi on the stove top according to the package directions. Drain in a colander and keep warm.

5. Remove the dish from the oven. Mix in the cooked gnocchi, feta, and basil, and serve.

6. Ingredient tip: You can substitute drained canned diced tomatoes for the chopped tomatoes. Look for low-sodium or no-salt-added canned tomatoes.

Nutrition:

Calories: 277; Total Fat: 7g; Saturated Fat: 2g; Cholesterol: 130mg; Sodium: 653mg; Total Carbohydrates: 35g; Fiber: 1g; Protein: 20g

Easiest Shrimp Scampi

Preparation Time: 15 minutes

Cooking Time: 1½ hours

Servings: 4

Ingredients:

- 1 lb. raw shrimp, peeled and deveined
- ¼ C. chicken broth
- 2 tbsp. butter
- 2 tbsp. olive oil
- 1 tbsp. fresh lemon juice
- 1 tbsp. garlic, minced
- 1 tbsp. dried parsley
- Salt and freshly ground black pepper, to taste

Directions:

1. In a slow cooker, place all the ingredients and stir to combine.
2. Set the slow cooker on "High" and cook, covered for about 1½ hours.
3. Uncover the slow cooker and stir the mixture.
4. Serve hot.

Nutrition:

Calories per serving: 252;

Carbohydrates: 2.6g;

Protein: 26.4g;

Fat: 14.8g;

Sugar: 0.2g;

Sodium: 406mg;

Fiber: 0.1g

Brown Rice Pilaf with Golden Raisins

Preparation Time: 5 minutes

Cooking Time: 15 minutes

Servings: 6

Ingredients:

- 1 tablespoon extra-virgin olive oil
- 1 cup chopped onion (about ½ medium onion)
- ½ cup shredded carrot (about 1 medium carrot)
- 1 teaspoon ground cumin
- ½ teaspoon ground cinnamon
- 2 cups instant brown rice
- 1¾ cups 100% orange juice
- ¼ cup water
- 1 cup golden raisins
- ½ cup shelled pistachios
- Chopped fresh chives (optional)

Directions:

1. In a medium saucepan over medium-high heat, heat the oil.
2. Add the onion and cook for 5 minutes, stirring frequently.
3. Add the carrot, cumin, and cinnamon, and cook for 1 minute, stirring frequently.

4. Stir in the rice, orange juice, and water. Bring to a boil, cover, then lower the heat to medium-low. Simmer for 7 minutes, or until the rice is cooked through and the liquid is absorbed.

5. Stir in the raisins, pistachios, and chives (if using) and serve.

Nutrition:

Calories: 320; Total Fat: 7g; Saturated Fat: 0g; Cholesterol: 0mg; Sodium: 37mg; Total Carbohydrates: 61g; Fiber: 5g; Protein: 6g

Slow Cooker Spanish Rice

Preparation Time: 10 minutes

Cooking Time: 4 hours 10 minutes

Servings: 8

Ingredients:

- Olive oil – 2 tablespoons, extra olive oil for crockpot greasing.
- Wholegrain rice – 2 cups
- Diced tomatoes in the can – 14½ ounces
- Medium yellow onion, chopped – 1
- Garlic, minced – 3 cloves
- Low-sodium broth or stock (chicken or vegetable), or water – 2 cups
- Red bell pepper, medium cut size – ½
- Yellow bell pepper, medium dice – ½
- Ground cumin – 1 ½ teaspoon
- Chili powder – 2 teaspoons
- Kosher salt – 1½ teaspoons
- Fresh cilantro leaves, for garnishing – 2 tablespoons

Directions:

1. Pour olive oil into a large skillet and bring it to medium heat.
2. Add rice into the skillet and combine well so that the grains get olive oil coating.

92

3. Now put the onion into the skillet and sauté for about 5 minutes, until the rice becomes pale golden brown.

4. Slightly grease the inside of crockpot with olive oil.

5. Transfer the browned rice to the crockpot.

6. Add broth, bell peppers, tomatoes, garlic, cumin, chili powder, salt and combine thoroughly.

7. Cover the crock, and slow cook for about 4 hours. Two hours later, check if the liquid is being absorbed by the rice well.

8. Continue cooking until the rice becomes soft and all the moisture gets absorbed.

9. Top it with cilantro leaves and serve hot.

Nutrition:

Calories: 55 ; Carbohydrates: 5.36g ; Fiber: 1.82g ; Protein: 1.01g; Cholesterol: 0g; Sugar: 2.31g; Fat: 3.78g; Sodium: 394.26mg

Triple-Green Pasta

Preparation Time: 5 minutes

Cooking Time: 15 minutes

Servings: 4

Ingredients:

- 8 ounces uncooked penne
- 1 tablespoon extra-virgin olive oil
- 2 garlic cloves, minced (1 teaspoon)
- ¼ teaspoon crushed red pepper
- 2 cups chopped fresh flat-leaf (Italian) parsley, including stems
- 5 cups loosely packed baby spinach (about 5 ounces)
- ¼ teaspoon ground nutmeg
- ¼ teaspoon freshly ground black pepper
- ¼ teaspoon kosher or sea salt
- 1/3 cup Castelvetrano olives (or other green olives), pitted and sliced (about 12)
- 1/3 Cup grated Pecorino Romano or Parmesan cheese (about 1 ounce)

Directions:

1. In a large stockpot, cook the pasta according to the package directions, but boil 1 minute less than instructed. Drain the pasta, and save ¼ cup of the cooking water.

2. While the pasta is cooking, in a large skillet over medium heat, heat the oil. Add the garlic and crushed red pepper, and cook for 30 seconds, stirring constantly. Add the parsley and cook for 1 minute, stirring constantly. Add the spinach, nutmeg, pepper, and salt, and cook for 3 minutes, stirring occasionally, until the spinach is wilted.

3. Add the pasta and the reserved ¼ cup pasta water to the skillet. Stir in the olives, and cook for about 2 minutes, until most of the pasta water has been absorbed. Remove from the heat, stir in the cheese, and serve.

Nutrition:

Calories: 271; Total Fat: 8g; Saturated Fat: 2g; Cholesterol: 5mg; Sodium: 345mg; Total Carbohydrates: 43g; Fiber: 10g; Protein: 15g

Eggroll in a bowl

Preparation Time: 10 minute

Cooking Time: 5 minutes

Servings: 3

Ingredients

- 1/2 cup of Green onions, needed to garnish
- 1 tablespoon of sesame oil
- 1/3 cup of soy sauce
- 1 teaspoon of ginger, should be minced
- 4 cloves of garlic, should be minced
- 12 ounces of shredded cabbage
- 1 1/2 pound of ground turkey breast

Directions:

1. Get a bowl and combine soy sauce, ginger, and garlic and put aside.
2. Set the turkey in a large skillet and apply medium heat to get it brown.
3. Next is to add the already shredded cabbage in it and stir very well to combine.
4. Then add the sauce mixture to the veggies and meat. Stir together and let it cook for about 3-5 minutes until the cabbage starts to wilt but remain crunchy
5. You can garnish with green onions if you like.

Nutrition:

Calories: 429

Protein: 52g

Total Carbohydrates: 27g

Sugars: 12g

Saturated Fat: 3g

Dessert

Berry Yogurt Trifle

Preparation Time: 15 minutes, plus 30 minutes to chill

Cooking Time: 0 minutes

Servings: 2

Ingredients:

- 2 cups nonfat vanilla Greek yogurt
- 2 tablespoons honey
- 1 (10-ounce) store-bought angel food cake, cut into 1-inch cubes
- 1½ cups strawberries, hulled and halved
- 1½ cups blueberries
- 1 cup Vanilla-Infused Whipped Cream

Directions:

1. In a small bowl, mix together the yogurt and honey.
2. In a large bowl or trifle dish, distribute half of the angel food cake in an even layer. Top the cake with 1 cup of the yogurt mixture, using a spatula to evenly coat. Top with half of the strawberries and blueberries. Repeat to make a second layer, then top with the whipped cream.
3. Cover and refrigerate to set, about 30 minutes.

Nutrition:

Calories: 243; Total fat 6g; Saturated Fat: 4g; Protein: 8g; Carbohydrates: 41 g; Fiber: 2g; Sodium: 291 mg

Vermicelli Pudding

Preparation Time: 10 minutes

Cooking Time: 45 minutes

Servings: 2

Ingredients:

- ½ Cup Vermicelli Noodles
- ½ Cup Sultans
- ½ Teaspoon Vanilla Extract, Pure
- ½ Teaspoon Nutmeg
- 1 Cup Milk
- 2 Tablespoons Sugar
- 2 Eggs

Directions:

1. Start by cooking your vermicelli noodles as your package dictates, and makes sure to drain them.
2. Whisk your eggs, milk and sugar in a bowl.
3. Add in your remaining ingredients.
4. Get out a baking dish and grease it. Place the mixture inside, and then bake at 320 for forty-five minutes.
5. Sprinkle with nutmeg before serving.

Nutrition:

Calories: 251; Protein: 11.6 Grams; Fat: 7.1 Grams; Carbs: 35.7 Grams ; Sodium: 120 mg

Strawberry Compote in Red Wine Syrup

Preparation Time: 10 minutes

Cooking Time: 20 minutes

Servings: 2

Ingredients:

- 1 cup red wine
- 1/3 Cup granulated sugar
- 1 teaspoon vanilla extract
- ½ teaspoon ground cinnamon
- 4 cups strawberries, hulled and sliced

Directions:

1. In a medium saucepan, bring the wine, sugar, vanilla, and cinnamon to a boil. Reduce heat and simmer until the liquid is reduced by half, about 20 minutes.
2. Place 1 cup of berries into each of 4 cups. Drizzle with 2 tablespoons of the red wine syrup.
3. Serve warm or chill in the refrigerator before serving.

Nutrition:

Calories: 119; Total Fat: 0g; Saturated Fat: 0g; Protein: 1g; Carbohydrates: 28g; Fiber: 3g; Sodium: 2mg

Homemade Caramel-Dipped Apples

Preparation Time: 10 minutes, plus 15 minutes to chill

Cooking Time: 1 minute

Servings: 2

Ingredients:

- 4 Pink Lady, Honeycrisp, Fuji, or Granny Smith apples
- Cooking spray
- ½ cup Homemade Caramel Sauce
- ½ cup unsalted peanuts, chopped

Directions:

1. Remove the stems of the apples, and push a wooden skewer into the bottom of each apple, about three quarters of the way through.
2. Line a baking sheet with parchment paper and coat with cooking spray.
3. Warm the caramel sauce in a microwave-safe bowl for 1 minute, stirring frequently.
4. Quickly roll each apple in the caramel sauce. Use a spoon to cover the apple with the sauce.
5. Roll or dip the caramel apples in the chopped nuts, then place on the prepared baking sheet.

Refrigerate until the caramel hardens, about 15 minutes.

Nutrition:

Calories: 311; Total Fat: 16g; Saturated Fat: 6g; Protein: 5g; Carbohydrates: 40g; Fiber: 6g; Sodium: 64mg

Pomegranate-Pistachio Bark

Preparation Time: 10 minutes, plus 45 minutes to chill

Cooking Time: 10 minutes

Servings: 2

Ingredients:

- ½ cup raw shelled pistachios, roughly chopped
- 1 pound 60% dark chocolate, broken into pieces
- ½ cup pomegranate arils, liquid drained
- 1/8 Teaspoon sea salt

Directions:

1. Line a baking sheet with parchment paper. Set aside.
2. Heat a small skillet over medium heat. Add the pistachios and cook until toasted, about 3 minutes. Set aside to cool.
3. In a small saucepan, bring a cup of water to a boil, then reduce heat to a simmer. Place a heat-proof medium bowl on top of the saucepan to make a double boiler. Add the chocolate to the bowl and cook, stirring gently with a wooden spoon until the mixture is smooth, about 5 minutes. Spoon the chocolate onto the prepared baking sheet, spreading to the edges evenly with a spatula.
4. Evenly sprinkle the chocolate with the pistachios, pomegranate arils, and sea salt.

5. Transfer the baking sheet to the refrigerator for about 45 minutes, until the chocolate sets.
6. Break the bark into 24 pieces and serve.

Nutrition:

Calories: 127; Total Fat: 8g; Saturated Fat: 4g; Protein: 2g; Carbohydrates: 11g; Fiber: 2g; Sodium: 13mg

CPSIA information can be obtained
at www.ICGtesting.com
Printed in the USA
LVHW052131240621
691049LV00003B/402